Exposing the Wickedness of the Sodomites and Defending the Reprobate Doctrine from the Holy Bible

By Alexander Larson

Introduction

It is quite unfortunate that in our modern society, people are becoming more accepting of the things which the Bible labels as abominable. This does not solely include those of the world, but also those who claim to be Christian, but who instead are entangled in the false doctrine of men. We should take heed to find refuge in the Word of God and shut out our ears to the lies of the world; as the Bible teaches, "We ought to obey God rather than man" (Acts 5:29).

As saved, born again, Bible-believing Christians, we should search the Scriptures diligently to discover the truth about the issues which underly our world today, regardless of the criticism we may receive for it. Persecution and hate can be expected from those who adhere to and preach the truth of God's word. As it is written,

> John 15:18-20 - If the world hate you, ye know that it hated me before it hated you. If ye were of the world, the world would love his own: but because ye are not of the world, but I have chosen you out of the world, therefore the world hateth you. Remember the word that I said unto you, The servant is not greater than his lord. If they have persecuted me, they will also persecute you; if they have kept my saying, they will keep yours also.

> 1 John 3:13 - Marvel not, my brethren, if the world hate you.

Just as the Pharisees attempted to shut up the mouth of Jesus, the false religious leaders and the serpents of today's world will shut up his servants. However, regardless of the opposition that we may receive, remember, God's word is the truth. Sometimes it may be difficult to swallow at first, or sometimes it may be hard to understand. However, as Christians, we should accept that God's word is the truth. The Bible says,

> John 8:47 - He that is of God heareth God's words: ye therefore hear them not, because ye are not of God.

> 2 Timothy 3:16 - All scripture is given by inspiration of God, and is profitable for doctrine, for reproof, for correction, for instruction in righteousness:

Matthew 4:4 - But he answered and said, It is written, Man shall not live by bread alone, but by every word that proceedeth out of the mouth of God.

Proverbs 30:5 - Every word of God is pure: he is a shield unto them that put their trust in him.

Those who are truly saved by putting their trust in Jesus Christ, God's word made flesh (John 1:14), will listen to the words of Christ, and be instructed in the teachings of the Bible. This is one of the primary doctrines of our faith, that we receive revelation and teaching by the Holy Spirit, through the reading of God's world, the Bible. Those who are truly right with God will manifest such in their attitude toward the wickedness of the world. The Bible says,

1 John 2:15-17 - Love not the world, neither the things that are in the world. If any man love the world, the love of the Father is not in him. 16 For all that is in the world, the lust of the flesh, and the lust of the eyes, and the pride of life, is not of the Father, but is of the world. 17 And the world passeth away, and the lust thereof: but he that doeth the will of God abideth for ever.

The lust of the flesh (fleshly lusts like fornicative and adulterous thoughts), the lust of the eyes (greed and covetousness), and the pride of life (exalting one's self, being proud and boastful): these things are wicked, and not of the Father. These things, all sins according to the Scriptures, will not have any place in the world to come.

In this essay, I shall endeavor to explain and expose the wickedness of a certain group of people, who demonstrate all of these three aspects of sin. These are the sodomites, or as they are called in modern vernacular, homosexuals. This seems to be a controversial subject today, especially as homosexuals gain increasing acceptance into society. Prior to 1962, sodomy was illegal in all 50 states of the U.S., while the final states to legalize sodomy, did so as late as 2003. Now, same-sex marriage is legal, and large corporations such a Google and Apple openly support the pride of these sinners during the so-called "Pride Month", in June. Even some churches now accept homosexuals, both to attend their churches, but also to be in leadership positions. This practice exists among denominations such as the Lutherans,

Episcopalians, Presbyterians, Congregationalists, and Methodists, among others. Adam Hamilton, the pastor of the 22,000 member "United Methodist Church of the Resurrection", openly affirms and supports homosexuality. Besides the stances of specific denominations, independent 'Christian' organizations are forming, such as "Born that Way Ministries", teaching that sodomy does not conflict with the Christian faith.

However, as will be demonstrated henceforth, the concept that sodomites belong anywhere near a church is foreign to Scripture. Instead, we learn from the Bible that homosexuality is a terrible sin, punishable by death under the Law of Moses, and that sodomites belong to a group of twisted, abominable people known as reprobates.

To understand this, we must first see what a reprobate is.

The Reprobate Doctrine

The word reprobate has several meanings in the English dictionary, one being "rejected as worthless or not standing a test: condemned" (Merriam-Webster). This meaning, a more archaic denotation of the term, fits with what the Bible teaches on reprobation. The KJV uses the word reprobate 7 times, but perhaps the most relevant and significant passage in the Bible which teaches the reprobate doctrine is Romans 1. Towards the end of the chapter, Paul explains the origin of reprobation and the fruit which it produces,

> Romans 1:18-32 - For the wrath of God is revealed from heaven against all ungodliness and unrighteousness of men, who hold the truth in unrighteousness; Because that which may be known of God is manifest in them; for God hath shewed it unto them. For the invisible things of him from the creation of the world are clearly seen, being understood by the things that are made, even his eternal power and Godhead; so that they are without excuse: Because that, when they knew God, they glorified him not as God, neither were thankful; but became vain in their imaginations, and their foolish heart was darkened. Professing themselves to be wise, they became fools, And changed the glory of the uncorruptible God into an image made like to corruptible man, and to birds, and fourfooted beasts, and creeping things. Wherefore God also gave them up to uncleanness through the lusts of their own hearts, to dishonour their own bodies between themselves: Who changed the truth of God into a lie, and worshipped and served the creature more than the Creator, who is blessed for ever. Amen. For this cause God gave them up unto vile affections: for even their women did change the natural use into that which is against nature: And likewise also the men, leaving the natural use of the woman, burned in their lust one toward another; men with men working that which is unseemly, and receiving in themselves that recompence of their error which was meet. And even as they did not like to retain God in their knowledge, God gave them over to a reprobate mind, to do those things which are not convenient; Being filled with all unrighteousness, fornication, wickedness, covetousness, maliciousness; full of envy, murder, debate, deceit, malignity;

whisperers, Backbiters, haters of God, despiteful, proud, boasters, inventors of evil things, disobedient to parents, Without understanding, covenantbreakers, without natural affection, implacable, unmerciful: Who knowing the judgment of God, that they which commit such things are worthy of death, not only do the same, but have pleasure in them that do them.

Because this is a long passage, we ought to break it down to get a closer look at what Paul is saying here. The word reprobate is found in verse 28, in the phrase "God gave them over to a reprobate mind." Why does God give some over to a reprobate mind? What exactly in this passage saying? Let's start with the first few verses:

Romans 1:18-19 - For the wrath of God is revealed from heaven against all ungodliness and unrighteousness of men, who hold the truth in unrighteousness; Because that which may be known of God is manifest in them; for God hath shewed it unto them.

So, the first characteristic of the subjects of this chapter is that these people who are ungodly and unrighteous have been shown the things of God. It's become manifest in them, so that they should not have a reason to deny the true God of the Bible. This speaks in part of those who have heard the Gospel, and thus have been presented with the knowledge of God through the preaching of his word. Romans 1 continues,

Romans 1:20-23 - For the invisible things of him from the creation of the world are clearly seen, being understood by the things that are made, even his eternal power and Godhead; so that they are without excuse: Because that, when they knew God, they glorified him not as God, neither were thankful; but became vain in their imaginations, and their foolish heart was darkened. Professing themselves to be wise, they became fools, And changed the glory of the uncorruptible God into an image made like to corruptible man, and to birds, and fourfooted beasts, and creeping things.

These next verses explain that the one true God should be the obvious truth for those who have heard the Gospel preached. Thus, they, unlike those who live in ignorance, are without excuse when they reject the Gospel and instead turn to idols. Another important passage on the doctrine of reprobation is 2

Peter 2, which also discusses the matter of those who have been presented with the Gospel, but who refuse to trust Christ -

> 2 Peter 2:20-21 - For if after they have escaped the pollutions of the world through the knowledge of the Lord and Saviour Jesus Christ, they are again entangled therein, and overcome, the latter end is worse with them than the beginning. For it had been better for them not to have known the way of righteousness, than, after they have known it, to turn from the holy commandment delivered unto them.

Here, it states that those who know the truth of the Lord and Saviour Christ, but who remain entangled in the world, are worse than ordinary unbelievers. Why? Because, as it says in Romans 1:20, "they are without excuse." Do not be mistaken about 2 Peter 2. False teachers will often twist this passage to teach that you can lose your salvation; however, nowhere does it mention those who are already saved. Rather, these are humans who have had the opportunity to become saved, and yet, they refuse to accept the Gospel and put their trust in Jesus. Instead, as it teaches in Romans 1, they continue in the religions of the world, worshipping the creature rather than the creator.

To help clarify the nature of these reprobates, let us look at an example of this first characteristic and step to becoming a reprobate. Suppose there is a man, of which age, it does not matter, who is by faith a Catholic. One day, a soulwinner bringing the Gospel of Christ, as it is written in the Bible, arrives at this Catholic's house. During this presentation of the Gospel, the soulwinner uses multiple Scriptures to show the Catholic that salvation is by faith alone in Christ, and not by the obeying the commandments and performing the sacraments, as the Roman Catholic religion teaches. This Catholic completely understands what the soulwinner is preaching. However, despite understanding the Gospel, and knowing that it is indeed what Christ and his apostles have spoken, he hardens his heart. He doesn't want to believe, so he rejects the whole concept in his heart and remains in the world.

Thus, the Catholic in this story has "that which may be known of God manifest" in him, "because God hath shown it to him" (v.19). And thus, he is "without excuse" (v. 20), and then, even though he knew God, he glorified him not as God, but become vain in his imaginations, and his foolish heart was darkened (v. 21-22). Thus, we see a progression of somebody into becoming a reprobate. Moving on, Romans 1 says,

> Romans 1:24-25 - Wherefore God also gave them up to uncleanness through the lusts of their own hearts, to dishonour their own bodies between themselves: Who changed the truth of God into a lie, and worshipped and served the creature more than the Creator, who is blessed for ever. Amen.

This passage shows a transition point for the reprobates. After denying the true God, and after rejecting the Gospel that has been presented to them, there comes a point when God gives them up instead. Moving on,

> Romans 1:26-28 - For this cause God gave them up unto vile affections: for even their women did change the natural use into that which is against nature: And likewise also the men, leaving the natural use of the woman, burned in their lust one toward another; men with men working that which is unseemly, and receiving in themselves that recompence of their error which was meet. And even as they did not like to retain God in their knowledge, <u>God gave them over to a reprobate mind</u>, to do those things which are not convenient.

This is perhaps the most controversial passage in the chapter, as this is when the issue of homosexuality is mentioned. Although the issue of homosexuality specifically will be addressed later, we must see how these sodomite reprobates are formed. From the previous verses, we see a progression from men being presented with the truth (v. 18-20), and then rejecting it in their heart and worshipping the things of this world rather than the true God (v. 21-25). Then, in verse 24, it's mentioned that "God also gave them up to uncleanness through the lusts of their own hearts." Here, in verse 26, it says "God gave them up unto vile affections," and in verse 28, that "God gave them over to a reprobate mind."

Modern Christianity widely rejects this Biblical principle. Instead, many modern denominations teach that God will never give up on you, and that there's always still hope for salvation. However, this passage teaches otherwise. Rather, those who have continuously rejected God's offer are themselves given up *by* God. God Himself is who initiates the final step, by rejecting them. Remember the definition of reprobate, "rejected as worthless or not standing a test: condemned." God has given them up, or in other words, rejected them.

In the next few verses, we see what becomes of the reprobates. The Bible says,

> Romans 1:29-32 - Being filled with all unrighteousness, fornication, wickedness, covetousness, maliciousness; full of envy, murder, debate, deceit, malignity; whisperers, Backbiters, haters of God, despiteful, proud, boasters, inventors of evil things, disobedient to parents, Without understanding, covenantbreakers, without natural affection, implacable, unmerciful: Who knowing the judgment of God, that they which commit such things are worthy of death, not only do the same, but have pleasure in them that do them.

This is the final characteristic of reprobates given in this chapter: that they are filled with all unrighteousness. Unlike ordinary unsaved people, who are sinners by nature, but who still by nature do the things contained in the law (Romans 2:14), these reprobates do not have any filter. Notice some of the things which are listed here: haters of God, without natural affection, unmerciful, etc. Reprobates, because they have refused to retain God in their knowledge, have received the punishment of destroying themselves in their sin. In verse 32, it mentions how these reprobates know also of the judgment of God and that they are worthy of death for these sins. Going back to the example of the Catholic from earlier: this man, who has become a reprobate, knew that he deserves death for his sin. He knows that he deserves the punishment of Hell for disobeying God. However, instead of trusting in Christ's atonement for his sins, he not only rejects the Gospel, but intentionally continues in his sins, and feels no guilt in doing them.

However, this is not an isolated doctrine. Other places in Scripture clearly show these same characteristics of reprobates. One of these is in 2 Timothy 3, where it says,

> 2 Timothy 3:1-8 - This know also, that in the last days perilous times shall come. For men shall be lovers of their own selves, covetous, boasters, proud, blasphemers, disobedient to parents, unthankful, unholy, Without natural affection, trucebreakers, false accusers, incontinent, fierce, despisers of those that are good, Traitors, heady, highminded, lovers of pleasures more than lovers of God; <u>Having a form of godliness, but denying the power thereof: from such turn away</u>. For of this sort are they which creep into houses, and lead captive silly women laden with sins, led away with divers lusts, <u>Ever</u>

learning, and never able to come to the knowledge of the truth. Now as Jannes and Jambres withstood Moses, so do these also resist the truth: men of corrupt minds, reprobate concerning the faith.

The attributes mentioned here are identical to those of Romans 1. First, the chapter starts off with a list of sins that reprobates partake in, which is very similar to that in Romans 1:29-31. In verse 5, it mentions that these men shall have "a form of godliness, but denying the power thereof: from such turn away." This refers to the fact that reprobates have been given the knowledge of the truth, but reject it. Even though they have a form of godliness (they've been presented with the Gospel), they deny the power of godliness. This is just as in Romans 1, where it says "Because that, when they knew God, they glorified him not as God," (v. 21). Another important component of verse 5 is that Paul advises us to turn away from these people. Why does he do this? Did not Jesus teach us to preach the Gospel throughout the world?

Mark 16:15 - And he said unto them, Go ye into all the world, and preach the gospel to every creature.

Why then, are we advised to turn away from people who have this form of godliness, but who deny the power thereof? The answer is simple: because they cannot be saved. This is explained later in the chapter, in verse 7, where it says that they are "ever learning, and never able to come to the knowledge of the truth." Never is an absolute. This means that these men, no matter how hard we try to give them the Gospel to get them saved, will never accept the knowledge which has been presented with them. Once they get to this state, there is no hope for them. They are, as it says in verse 8, "reprobate concerning the faith", or in other words, they've been rejected from our religion. It is impossible for them to understand Scripture.

We see an example of this in the Gospels, where Jesus is asked why he speaks in parables around the multitudes. It is a Biblical principle that the natural, unsaved person cannot understand the things of God (1 Cor. 2:14), and thus, it must be explained to them. We see an example of this in Acts 8, where the Ethiopian eunuch says to Philip, who asks him if he understands the scroll of Isaiah, "How can I, except some man should guide me" (v. 31)? In other words, those who are unsaved must have somebody explain the words of God to them. They cannot simply read the Bible and figure it out on their own. Jesus said,

Matthew 13:10-15 - And the disciples came, and said unto him, Why speakest thou unto them in parables? He answered and said unto them, Because it is given unto you to know the mysteries of the kingdom of heaven, but to them it is not given. For whosoever hath, to him shall be given, and he shall have more abundance: but whosoever hath not, from him shall be taken away even that he hath. <u>Therefore speak I to them in parables: because they seeing see not; and hearing they hear not, neither do they understand</u>. And in them is fulfilled the prophecy of Esaias, which saith, By hearing ye shall hear, and shall not understand; and seeing ye shall see, and shall not perceive: <u>For this people's heart is waxed gross, and their ears are dull of hearing, and their eyes they have closed; lest at any time they should see with their eyes and hear with their ears, and should understand with their heart, and should be converted, and I should heal them</u>.

Not only is Jesus acknowledging the fact that the unsaved cannot understand the words of God, but he is taking it a step further by explaining that there are some among the multitude who, although hearing the word of God preached, will purposely shut it from their minds and refuse to believe. Thus, Jesus, foreknowing that there are some of these among the multitudes, he explains that their ears are dull of hearing and their eyes are closed "lest at any time they should see...and should be converted, and I should heal them." Essentially, Jesus is teaching that those who will not be saved cannot be given the mysteries of the kingdom of heaven, because they've already had their heart hardened.

This is perhaps a reference to reprobation, in that, like the subjects in 2 Timothy 3, the change in their heart has prohibited them from coming to the knowledge of the truth. One thing which we must understand when it comes to the reprobate doctrine is that rejection is a state which is given from God. Although it is by the person's own free will to reject God and the Gospel at first, because of their hate for the truth, God is the one who puts them in this state. Remember, in Romans 1, it says "God gave them up to uncleanness through the lusts of their own hearts," (v. 24), "God gave them up unto vile affections," (v. 26), and "God gave them over to a reprobate mind" (v. 28). It is God who gives them up, and gives them over.

We see an example of this in the story of the Pharaoh of Egypt, who at first hardens his heart, but whose heart is later hardened by God. This, and other examples of reprobates in the Bible, shall be discussed later in this essay. It is God's decision to reject them, thus making it impossible for them to come to the knowledge of the truth. The Bible teaches this in reference to the end times, saying,

> 2 Thessalonians 2:9-12 - Even him, whose coming is after the working of Satan with all power and signs and lying wonders, And with all deceivableness of unrighteousness in them that perish; because they received not the love of the truth, that they might be saved. <u>And for this cause God shall send them strong delusion, that they should believe a lie:</u> That they all might be damned who believed not the truth, but had pleasure in unrighteousness.

Here, we see all of the characteristics of a reprobate once again. In verse 10, it mentions that those who perish with the Man of Sin (the subject of the chapter), are those who "received not the love of the truth." In verse 11, it goes on to say that because of their rejection of the Gospel, because they refused to believe the truth, but instead changed the truth of God into a lie, GOD sends them a strong delusion. Again, God makes the final decision. Once somebody has crossed the line with God, they will never step back over, because they cannot. Remember, 2 Timothy 3:7 says that they are "ever learning, but never able to come to the knowledge of the truth." This above passage ends with a definitive punishment for those who end up believing the lie: they all are damned.

This is consistent with the Book of Revelation's teaching on the Mark of the Beast. Since 2 Thessalonians 2 is in the context of the Antichrist, it's crucial to understand how the coming of the Antichrist relates to people becoming reprobate. One of the three angels in Revelation 14 pronounces this frightening warning:

> Revelation 14:9-11 - And the third angel followed them, saying with a loud voice, If any man worship the beast and his image, and receive his mark in his forehead, or in his hand, The same shall drink of the wine of the wrath of God, which is poured out without mixture into the cup of his indignation; <u>and he shall be tormented with fire and brimstone in the presence of the holy angels, and in the presence of the Lamb:</u> And the smoke of their torment ascendeth up for ever and ever: and

they have no rest day nor night, who worship the beast and his image, and <u>whosoever receiveth the mark of his name.</u>

Just as the word "whosoever" means anybody in John 3:16, whosoever means the same thing here. Every person, no matter what they do, who receives the Mark of the Beast will go to hell, and burn for eternity in the Lake of Fire. They are damned, and that's it, without exception. Thus, those who accept the Mark are by action rejecting God, and thus, become reprobate. As the day draws nearer, it's becoming clear that more and more people have already descended into this irreversible state. The Bible prophesies this, saying,

> 1 Timothy 4:1-4 - Now the Spirit speaketh expressly, <u>that in the latter times</u> some shall depart from the faith, giving heed to seducing spirits, and doctrines of devils; 2 Speaking lies in hypocrisy; <u>having their conscience seared with a hot iron</u>; 3 Forbidding to marry, and commanding to abstain from meats, which God hath created to be received with thanksgiving of them which believe and know the truth. 4 For every creature of God is good, and nothing to be refused, if it be received with thanksgiving:

These doctrines listed here are not just any false doctrines: they're labelled as doctrines of devils. Celibacy and forced vegetarianism are two of these doctrines which do not originate from God. However, setting aside the specific doctrines, one phrase within this passage that we should take heed to is "having their conscience seared with a hot iron." What does this mean? The Bible explains what our conscience is elsewhere, saying,

> Romans 2:14-15 - For when the Gentiles, which have not the law, do by nature the things contained in the law, these, having not the law, are a law unto themselves: 15 Which shew the work of the law written in their hearts, their <u>conscience</u> also bearing witness, and their thoughts the mean while accusing or else excusing one another;)

The word conscience is from the root word science, meaning 'knowledge,' and the prefix con-, meaning 'with.' This refers to the inherent knowledge of what's right and wrong which is given to mankind. Even the Gentiles, who do not have the law of Moses, are able to figure out that murder, theft, adultery, and the like are wicked. This is because God has given everybody a conscience, as it explains in the above passage. This is the nature of mankind, that we do the things contained in the law, even when we do not have knowledge of the law. When Adam and Eve sinned in the Garden of Eden, they did so by eating of the tree of the knowledge of good and evil (Genesis 3:5-7). Thus, their eyes were opened, and that which is righteous and that which is unrighteous became known unto mankind.

However, reprobates do not have this gift, and instead have their conscience "seared with a hot iron" as it explains in 1 Timothy 4:2. These doctrines of devils are not only in their mind, but it has become part of their conscience. Another passage about reprobation delves further into this teaching, saying,

> Titus 1:15-16 - Unto the pure all things are pure: but unto them that are defiled and unbelieving is nothing pure; but even their mind and conscience is defiled. They profess that they know God; but in works they deny him, being abominable, and disobedient, and unto every good work reprobate.

This now speaks of reprobates as having "their mind and conscience" defiled. This passage also shows us how many false prophets are reprobates, teaching of those who profess God, but who cannot be obedient in God on account of their inward rejection of him. Going back to the example from earlier of the Catholic who rejected the Gospel presented to him by a soulwinner; this Catholic may profess to be a man of God, but in reality, he, in knowledge of the truth, directly opposes God by continuing in the evil deeds of his false church. Once somebody rejects God, and they are in turn rejected, their conscience, being defiled, no longer can distinguish between right and wrong, good and evil. They cannot do any good work.

One of the ways which reprobation also can occur is by blasphemy of the Holy Spirit. It has already been demonstrated that one becomes reprobate after being rejected by God and being given over to the reprobate mind. This is a result of the man's initial decision to deny the knowledge of the truth and turn away from the Gospel. However, blasphemy of the Holy Ghost, known also as the "Unforgivable Sin", is an action which also causes reprobation. Jesus said,

> Matthew 12:31-32 - Wherefore I say unto you, All manner of sin and blasphemy shall be forgiven unto men: but the blasphemy against the Holy Ghost shall not be forgiven unto men. 32 And whosoever speaketh

> a word against the Son of man, it shall be forgiven him: but whosoever speaketh against the Holy Ghost, it shall not be forgiven him, neither in this world, neither in the world to come.

> Luke 12:10 - And whosoever shall speak a word against the Son of man, it shall be forgiven him: but unto him that blasphemeth against the Holy Ghost it shall not be forgiven.

> Mark 3:28-29 - Verily I say unto you, All sins shall be forgiven unto the sons of men, and blasphemies wherewith soever they shall blaspheme: But he that shall blaspheme against the Holy Ghost hath never forgiveness, but is in danger of eternal damnation.

Thus, if you blaspheme the Holy Ghost, as these Pharisees did by calling God's spirit the Devil, you cannot be saved. Salvation itself is being saved from your sin (Matt. 1:21), through the forgiveness of your sins (Rom. 3:25). Since the wages of sin is death (Rom. 6:23), without the remission of these sins, one cannot escape the punishment of death and hell. Thus, once somebody blasphemes the Holy Ghost, there is never hope for salvation for them. They are become rejected by God.

This flies in the face of the doctrine of many modern Christians, who accept everybody, and attempt to bring the Gospel to all people, expecting a chance even with those who have hardened their hearts and shut up their ears past the point of even considering acknowledgment of the truth. Another way in which somebody could become reprobate is by rejecting God's Word, a subject which has already been discussed. As it states in Romans 1:19 and 2 Peter 2:21, the knowledge of God and of the Lord and Saviour Jesus Christ has been delivered to them, but they have denied it. The Bible also says,

> Jeremiah 6:10 - To whom shall I speak, and give warning, that they may hear? behold, their ear is uncircumcised, and they cannot hearken: behold, the word of the Lord is unto them a reproach; they have no delight in it.

> Zechariah 7:12 - Yea, they made their hearts as an adamant stone, lest they should hear the law, and the words which the Lord of hosts hath sent in his spirit by the former prophets: therefore came a great wrath from the Lord of hosts.

These two passages once again touch on the subject that it is impossible for the reprobates to come to the knowledge of the truth. Instead, they've hardened their hearts so much that "they cannot hearken." This does not say "they will not hearken", but rather "they cannot." Such is the same to those who have no delight in the Word of God, but have denied it in their heart. Compare the words of Zechariah 7:12 with that of Jesus' explanation of why he speaks in parables in Matthew 13. Both reveal that there exists a certain group of people, who no matter what, will never hearken to the word of God, lest they should listen to the rebuke of the Lord. There is no denying that in this world, there simply exist some who do not only not care about the Bible, but who also actively hate and oppose the Scripture, and resist and reject God and his grace.

The rejection of his word can also lead to several dangerous activities from which there is no return. The Bible teaches us not to alter the words of God, and that those who are unsaved who do so shall never have salvation -

> Revelation 22:18-19 - For I testify unto every man that heareth the words of the prophecy of this book, If any man shall add unto these things, God shall add unto him the plagues that are written in this book: And if any man shall take away from the words of the book of this prophecy, God shall take away his part out of the book of life, and out of the holy city, and from the things which are written in this book.

Thus, anybody who takes away the words from the Book of Revelation, to alter the prophecy which God has given, has no hope of being saved. Tampering with God's word is serious, and something which God does not take lightly. Those who write and publish false Bible versions such as the NLT and "The Message" which radically change God's word by adding and subtracting from it, have already had their names blotted out of the Book of Life. They have become rejected by God and are not applicable for grace.

This is the frightening truth, whether it pleases you or not. Over and over again, we see passages discussing this subset of people who, by denying the one true God in their hearts, and by rejecting his word and his clear doctrine, have been themselves rejected by the Creator, and given over to a reprobate mind. Their conscience is defiled by the hardness of their heart, and it becomes impossible for them to believe the truth, to understand God's word, and to feel remorse for their wicked actions (which are manifold: as it is written, "They are filled with all unrighteousness"). Christians need to stop assuming that there is no line to be crossed.

The Bible even shows us examples of people throughout history who are reprobates, who have gone past the point of no return. These characters display all of the same attributes and characteristics as what is discussed of a reprobate in Romans 1, 2 Timothy 3, and Titus 1. One of the most significant examples of a reprobate in the Bible is that of the Pharaoh of Egypt during the period of the Exodus. For those who are not familiar with the story, the Pharaoh, who was probably called Dedumose by name, ruled over the Hebrews when God's prophet Moses came to free the children of Israel from captivity in Egypt. In order to convince the Pharaoh to release the Israelites, God sent ten plagues upon Egypt. However, each time, instead of listening to the warning and accepting the sovereignty of God, the Pharaoh hardened his heart and refused to let the Israelites grow.

This process is shown within the Book of Exodus. At first, after seeing the miracles of God through Moses, Pharoah hardened his own heart, and rejected the true God by his own mind. First, God prophesies that Pharaoh will not repent at the signs of the plagues, but instead, will refuse to listen.

> Exodus 7:3-4 - And I will harden Pharaoh's heart, and multiply my signs and my wonders in the land of Egypt. But Pharaoh shall not hearken unto you, that I may lay my hand upon Egypt, and bring forth mine armies, and my people the children of Israel, out of the land of Egypt by great judgments.

Then, we see a progression, where at first, Pharaoh hardens his own heart.

> Exodus 7:13-14 - And he hardened Pharaoh's heart, that he hearkened not unto them; as the Lord had said. And the Lord said unto Moses, Pharaoh's heart is hardened, he refuseth to let the people go.

> Exodus 7:22 - And the magicians of Egypt did so with their enchantments: and Pharaoh's heart was hardened, neither did he hearken unto them; as the Lord had said.

> Exodus 8:15 - But when Pharaoh saw that there was respite, he hardened his heart, and hearkened not unto them; as the Lord had said.

Exodus 8:19 - Then the magicians said unto Pharaoh, This is the finger of God: and Pharaoh's heart was hardened, and he hearkened not unto them; as the Lord had said.

Exodus 8:32 - And Pharaoh hardened his heart at this time also, neither would he let the people go.

Exodus 9:7 - And Pharaoh sent, and, behold, there was not one of the cattle of the Israelites dead. And the heart of Pharaoh was hardened, and he did not let the people go.

Each of these examples of Pharaoh hardening his heart takes place after a miracle or plague which Pharaoh can clearly see, but which he does not ascribe to the God of Israel. The first time, after Aaron's rod becomes a serpent. The second time, after the plague of blood. The third time, after the plague of frogs. The fourth time, the plague of lice. The fifth time, the plague of flies. The sixth time, the plague of the livestock. Then, a change takes place after the plague of boils, the sixth of the Ten Plagues.

Exodus 9:12 - And the Lord hardened the heart of Pharaoh, and he hearkened not unto them; as the Lord had spoken unto Moses.

This is the first time in which it is explicitly mentioned that the LORD hardens Pharaoh's heart. This is mentioned several more times, such as in Exodus 10:1, 10:20, 10:27, 11:10, and 14:8. Why is there a sudden change? Because, even in the Old Testament, we see the reprobate doctrine. Recall Romans 1, that this same progression is revealed. First, people are given the knowledge of the truth, and see the clear hand of God upon the world (v. 18-20). Then, they reject what has been shown to them, and harden their heart, refusing to give glory to the true God (v. 21-25). Thus, God gives them up and over to a reprobate mind himself (v. 24, 26, 28). This is exactly what happened to Pharaoh. After seeing the power of God unleashed upon his people, his wicked heart became so hardened that there came a point when God took control, and gave him up by his own power.

There are several other examples of reprobates in the Bible. One of the titles given to them in the Old Testament is "sons of Belial". The Hebrew word belial (בְּ֯לִ֗יַ֯עַל), from which this name comes, literally means "worthless."

In the New Testament, Belial is a name given to Satan himself, as a contrast with Christ:

> 2 Corinthians 6:14-15 - Be ye not unequally yoked together with unbelievers: for what fellowship hath righteousness with unrighteousness? and what communion hath light with darkness? <u>And what concord hath Christ with Belial</u>? or what part hath he that believeth with an infidel?

So, those called "sons of Belial", are literally the "sons of worthlessness." Some of the people mentioned in Scripture with this title include the sons of Eli.

> 1 Samuel 2:12 - Now the sons of Eli were sons of Belial; they knew not the Lord.

Later in the chapter, it mentions that Eli's sons did sin which was "very great before the LORD (v. 17)," and that they "lay with women that assembled at the door of the tabernacle of the congregation (v. 22)." However, a much clearer example is that of Nabal of Maon, discussed in 1 Samuel 25:

> 1 Samuel 25:17 - Now therefore know and consider what thou wilt do; for evil is determined against our master, and against all his household: for he is such a son of Belial, that a man cannot speak to him.

The last phrase "that a man cannot speak to him" is possibly in reference to the fact that reprobates are "never able to come to the knowledge of the truth (2 Tim. 3:7)." Thus, it is impossible to convince this man, Nabal, to follow after the Lord. Earlier in the chapter, in verse 3, it describes Nabal as "churlish and evil in his doings." When Nabal dies towards the end of the chapter, David praises God for smiting Nabal, saying,

> 1 Samuel 25:39 - And when David heard that Nabal was dead, he said, Blessed be the Lord, that hath pleaded the cause of my reproach from the hand of Nabal, and hath kept his servant from evil: for the Lord hath returned the wickedness of Nabal upon his own head. And David sent and communed with Abigail, to take her to him to wife.

Why would David praise the Lord for doing such a thing? David gave respect even to Saul, who became wicked in his latter days, and who tried to kill David. The reason why is because David recognized that this man of Belial was pure evil, a person who rejected God in totality. Remember, Belial means "worthless." It's a false doctrine to teach that everybody is inherently equal and each person has the hope for salvation. Some have already been given a chance, but because of their wickedness, have been shut out from the hope of eternal life. These haters of God shall be discussed later, but first, I want to briefly discuss that reprobation is something which is well known and seen even in our modern world. The difference is that it's often called by a different name.

To the psychologists and scientists of the world, what a Bible-believing Christian would call a reprobate is called a 'psychopath.' In colloquial usage, this word is usually just forced onto insane people. However, as a medical term, psychopathy is an actual identifiable condition with certain characteristics. According to the *Psychology Today* article titled "Psychopathy", psychopaths "lack conscience and empathy, making him manipulative, volatile, and often criminal."

The US National Library of Medicine article titled "Psychopathy: Cognitive and Neural Dysfunction" defines psychopathy as "a disorder characterized by pronounced emotional deficits, marked by reduction in guilt and empathy, and involves increased risk for displaying antisocial behavior" (R. James Blair, *Dialgoues in Clinical Neuroscience*). Science Direct defines psychopathy as "a mental (antisocial) disorder in which an individual manifests amoral and antisocial behavior, shows a lack of ability to love or establish meaningful personal relationships, expresses extreme egocentricity, and demonstrates a failure to learn from experience and other behaviors associated with the condition."

So, it's clear what psychopathy is: simply the modern medical term for reprobation. The Bible shows us that these reprobates, when given over to their reprobate mind, are filled with "all unrighteousness (Romans 1:29)." While ordinary unsaved people have the ability to distinguish between what's right and wrong, as they have the conscience God has given to them (Romans 2:14-15), psychopath reprobates do not have any empathy or understanding of morality. They have become total evil, humans with a defiled conscience and mind. It's this disorder known today as psychopathy which has given rise to disgusting serial killers such as Ted Bundy, Jeffrey Dahmer, and John Wayne Gacy, who all felt no remorse for their wicked sins.

To understand the connection between psychopathy and reprobation further, I suggest watching the documentary "Psychopath Reprobates", which specifically deals with the link between psychopaths and reprobates.

So, it's become abundantly clear that God has rejected some, and given them over to the reprobate mind described in the Bible. We see that there exist some people who love being in darkness so much, that they refuse to believe the witness which God has given to us, and turn away from the Gospel delivered unto them. They turn to the religions of the world, even when having the knowledge of what's right. Upon stepping across this line, God gives them over to a reprobate mind, which defiles their conscience. They thus no longer feel guilt, and have an apathetic attitude towards sin. These people are filled with all unrighteousness, unable to be brought to salvation, and are thus worthless, and worthy of more judgment than those in ignorance. Whether it's pleasant to hear or not, this is the truth of the matter.

Returning to the praise from David to God regarding the death of Nabal: what warrants such hate for this man? Does not the Bible also teach that we should love everybody? This is what some Christians will teach and believe. However, the Bible in no way supports this. Rather, we are to love our own personal enemies, as Jesus has commanded in Matthew 5:44. However, this is referring to those who persecute YOU, who oppose YOU, who hate YOU. This is what the passage puts emphasis on,

> Matthew 5:44 - But I say unto you, Love your enemies, bless them that curse you, do good to them that hate you, and pray for them which despitefully use you, and persecute you;

However, the Bible contrasts this with the hatred of God. The Bible says,

> Psalm 139:21-22 - Do not I hate them, O Lord, that hate thee? and am not I grieved with those that rise up against thee? I hate them with perfect hatred: I count them mine enemies.

The Bible teaches that there is a time to love, and a time to hate (Ecclesiastes 3:8). This is different from doing good unto those who are personally transgressing against you. Rather, we are to hate those who hate and oppose God. This includes reprobates. One of the sins listed among those which reprobates perform is the hatred of God:

> Romans 1:29-30 - Being filled with all unrighteousness, fornication, wickedness, covetousness, maliciousness; full of envy, murder, debate, deceit, malignity; whisperers, Backbiters, haters of God, despiteful, proud, boasters, inventors of evil things, disobedient to parents,

The reprobates are haters of God. Thus, like David, who hates those who hate the LORD, it is acceptable for us, as lovers of God, to oppose and hate these reprobates. They are worthless, children of the devil, those who make it their goal to send people to hell. It is foolish to say that hate whatsoever is wicked, for even God hates some of the wicked, as it teaches in Psalm 5:5, Psalm 10:3, Proverbs 6:19, Leviticus 26:30, Hosea 9:15, among other Scriptures. Reprobates are the enemies of God, the servants of the Devil.

The Homosexuals

What does any of this have to do with homosexuality? Why would I talk about these reprobates specifically, those who have completely rejected God in their hearts, and who have turned away from the saving grace of God? The Bible mentions homosexuals and homosexual acts in various places, explaining how these things come about, and what the punishment for these actions are. First, it should be established that homosexual intercourse is an abominable sin in the Law of Moses:

> Leviticus 18:22 - Thou shalt not lie with mankind, as with womankind: it is abomination.

> Leviticus 20:13 - If a man also lie with mankind, as he lieth with a woman, both of them have committed an abomination: they shall surely be put to death; their blood shall be upon them.

Homosexuality is not just a minor sin; it is held on the same level as other sexual immorality, and is punishable thus by death. Not only this, but in both of these commandments, a man lying with a man is classified as an "abomination." The word abomination is defined as "a thing that causes disgust or hatred." The action of having two same-sex people have intercourse is hated and detested by God. It's not just a minor sin. Other sins which are considered abominations in the Bible include idolatry (Deut. 7:25), prostitution (Deut. 23:8), child sacrifice (Jer. 32:35), murder, adultery (Jer. 7:9-10), among other wicked sins. This is not a light commandment.

In addition, Leviticus 20:13 gives the punishment of death for men who lie with mankind. This is the same level of punishment as those who commit murder, adultery, blasphemy, and the like. Now, before moving past this point: there exist some who twist the above verses to try to teach that these are not talking about homosexuals (despite the clear fact that it mentions men lying with men). Often, these people use other Bible versions which change mentions of sodomites to that of temple prostitutes specifically. However, there is no indication of such in the text. The Hebrew word translated as "lie" in Leviticus 18:22 and 20:13, is yishkab (יִשְׁכַּב), which is the same word used in the story of Lot's daughters in Genesis 19:

> Genesis 19:32-33, 36 - Come, let us make our father drink wine, and we will <u>lie</u> with him, that we may preserve seed of our father. And they made their father drink wine that night: and the firstborn went in, and lay with her father; and he perceived not when she lay down, nor when she arose... Thus were both the daughters of Lot with child by their father.

Thus, we can see that this word refers to sexual intercourse, as it produces children. So, in the Leviticus commandments, the phrase is saying, in other words, "If a man also has sexual intercourse with man, as he has sexual intercourse with a woman..." There is no mention of prostitution specifically, but rather, an absolute of all homosexuals is given. There should be no doubt from these passages that homosexuality is wicked in the eyes of God.

Additionally, beyond these two commandments, there are also several examples and stories of people performing these abominations in the Bible. The most well known of these is the story of Sodom and Gomorrah. From here comes the term 'sodomite,' a biblical term which refers to homosexuals. The Bible says,

> Genesis 19:4-10 - But before they lay down, <u>the men of the city</u>, even the men of Sodom, compassed the house round, both old and young, all the people from every quarter: And they called unto Lot, and said unto him, Where are the men which came in to thee this night? bring them out unto us, <u>that we may know them.</u> And Lot went out at the

door unto them, and shut the door after him, And said, I pray you, brethren, <u>do not so wickedly</u>. Behold now, I have two daughters which have not known man; let me, I pray you, bring them out unto you, and do ye to them as is good in your eyes: only unto these men do nothing; for therefore came they under the shadow of my roof. And they said, Stand back. And they said again, This one fellow came in to sojourn, and he will needs be a judge: <u>now will we deal worse with thee, than with them.</u> And they pressed sore upon the man, even Lot, and came near to break the door. But the men put forth their hand, and pulled Lot into the house to them, and shut to the door.

To summarize, these men of Sodom come to Lot's house, demanding to "know" the two angels who came into Lot's house. This is not a friendly greeting. The word know here is the same as in Genesis 4:1 - "And Adam knew Eve his wife, and she conceived, and bare Cain." This phrase once again refers to sexual intercourse. The men of Sodom wished to do this to the two visiting men. Lot responds strongly by telling them to "do not so wickedly." This is not just a minor offense. In the previous chapter, God says,

> Genesis 18:20 - And the Lord said, Because the cry of Sodom and Gomorrah is great, and because their sin is <u>very grievous</u>;

One of the sins of Sodom was homosexuality, as we see in this story. Notice also how that those who beat at Lot's door threaten to do even worse to Lot because of his criticism of their actions. This demonstrates their unbridledness. Because of the sin of these cities, they are overthrown and destroyed by God, through fire and brimstone. The story continues by saying,

> Genesis 19:24-25 - Then the Lord rained upon Sodom and upon Gomorrah brimstone and fire from the Lord out of heaven; And he overthrew those cities, and all the plain, and all the inhabitants of the cities, and that which grew upon the ground.

Thus Sodom was destroyed for their wickedness. However, this is not the last mention of Sodom and Gomorrah in the Bible. The Bible continues to use these cities as examples of the judgment of God and as a sample of wickedness. For example, in the Book of Isaiah, one of the attributes of Sodom listed is that its inhabitants didn't even hide their sin, saying,

> Isaiah 3:9 - The shew of their countenance doth witness against them; and they declare their sin as Sodom, they hide it not. Woe unto their soul! for they have rewarded evil unto themselves.

Additionally, in the New Testament, Sodom and Gomorrah are mentioned several times when discussing the subject of God's judgment.

> 2 Peter 2:6 - And turning the cities of Sodom and Gomorrha into ashes condemned them with an overthrow, making them an ensample unto those that after should live ungodly;

> Jude 1:7 - Even as Sodom and Gomorrha, and the cities about them in like manner, giving themselves over to fornication, and going after strange flesh, are set forth for an example, suffering the vengeance of eternal fire.

The destruction of these cities are an example of how God deals with their specific sins, which are even mentioned in Jude 1:7. Besides fornication is general (which is a generic term for all sexual immorality), it states that those in the cities went after "strange flesh." This is no doubt referring to the homosexual acts mentioned in Genesis 19, that the men of Sodom lusted after the men who came into the city. From this event comes the term "sodomite", which is used 5 times in the KJV. One of the occurences is within another commandment of the Torah, which says,

> Deuteronomy 23:17-18 - There shall be no whore of the daughters of Israel, nor a sodomite of the sons of Israel. Thou shalt not bring the hire of a whore, or the price of a dog, into the house of the Lord thy God for any vow: for even both these are abomination unto the Lord thy God.

Notice how in verse 17, both the whore and the sodomite are mentioned; in the next verse, it mentions the "hire of a whore, or the price of a dog." So, sodomites are compared with dogs, which are mentioned among unclean animals in Leviticus 11. I shall discuss why sodomites are also called dogs in this passage momentarily. However, first we should examine another passage in the Bible which gives an example of homosexual activity. The Bible says,

> Judges 19:22-23 - Now as they were making their hearts merry, behold, the men of the city, certain sons of Belial, beset the house round about,

and beat at the door, and spake to the master of the house, the old man, saying, <u>Bring forth the man that came into thine house, that we may know him.</u> And the man, the master of the house, went out unto them, and said unto them, Nay, my brethren, nay, I pray you, <u>do not so wickedly</u>; seeing that this man is come into mine house, do not this folly.

This story is similar to what happened in Sodom. Men of this city, Gibeah, approach this house and demand to know the visitor. The master of the house replies in the same way Lot did, saying "do not so wickedly." Notice also that these men of the city are called "sons of Belial" in this passage. Remember, this denotes them as children of worthlessness, and as reprobates. Besides these men being sodomites, they are also shown to be reprobates. However, is this just a coincidence?

We shall see shortly that the mention of these men being sons of Belial is not a minor detail. Rather, this passage, along with several others, demonstrate a plain truth about homosexuals. Despite what the world teaches us, sodomites are not normal, and they are not born with a same-sex affinity. Rather, homosexuality is a state, a characteristic, which only exists because of reprobation. They fall into this unclean lust because of their rejection of God, because they become haters of God. Homosexuality is not just an ordinary sin; it is a perverse crime of the reprobates.

The principal passage on reprobation, Romans 1, deals with this specifically. We skipped over it earlier to focus on the reprobate doctrine specifically, but sodomy is evidently a sin connected with God's rejection. The Bible says,

Romans 1:26-32 - For this cause God gave them up unto vile affections: <u>for even their women did change the natural use into that which is against nature: And likewise also the men, leaving the natural use of the woman, burned in their lust one toward another; men with men working that which is unseemly,</u> and receiving in themselves that recompence of their error which was meet. And even as they did not like to retain God in their knowledge, God gave them over to a reprobate mind, to do those things which are not convenient; Being filled with all unrighteousness, fornication, wickedness, covetousness, maliciousness; full of envy, murder, debate, deceit, malignity; whisperers, Backbiters, haters of God, despiteful, proud, boasters, inventors of evil things, disobedient to parents, Without understanding, covenantbreakers, without natural affection, implacable, unmerciful: Who knowing the judgment of God, that they which commit such things are worthy of death, not only do the same, but have pleasure in them that do them.

The very first thing mentioned in this passage which is a characteristic of reprobates is women lusting after women and men lusting after men. This is not separating to talking about a separate group of people; rather, it is continuing to talk to us about the reprobates. First, we see the phrase "for this cause." This refers to the context of people rejecting God despite having that which is known of God manifest in them. Then, because of this, God gave them up to vile affections: which specifically refers to homosexuality, as stated in verses 26 and 27. Thus, we see that the only reason why sodomites exist in the first place is because they have rejected God. They are not born as homosexuals, but rather, they become one after rejecting God's word. In verse 28, it is written that "they did not like to retain God in their knowledge." The word they, being a pronoun, requires an antecedent, or a previously mentioned subject. This, of course, is referring to the sodomites mentioned in the previous verses.

It should also be considered that an attribute of reprobation is being filled with all unrighteousness, as it mentions in verse 29, before listing off a multitude of sins. Do not be deceived by the world. Sodomites are filled with a myriad of wickednesses. It's not just their sexual immorality, but they're also haters of God, haters of their parents, unmerciful, murderers, etc. This is what the Bible says. This is what we ought to believe, regardless of how offensive we perceive it to be.

This is why Judges 19 calls the men of Gibeah "sons of Belial", because they were only homosexuals on account of their reprobation. This is why Isaiah 3:9 mentions that the people of Sodom did not hide their sins. They have no moral compass, no conscience. They do not even have shame for this sin. This is why the sodomites are called dogs in Deuteronomy 23. A dog will hump anything. A dog does not simply restrict itself to one partner like a godly person does. A dog is "without natural affection." A dog is a filthy animal, according to the Bible. The Bible says,

Job 14:4 - Who can bring a clean thing out of an unclean? not one.

It is foolish to think that sodomites can be brought towards the light. They have rejected God, and God has given them over to a reprobate mind. That transition is what transformed these faggots into what they are (by the way, the term faggot is certainly appropriate for homosexuals; the word means a bundle of sticks. Just like a faggot is used as fuel for a fire, these faggots will one day be bundled together and thrown into the Lake of Fire). That is why the Bible simply tells us to kill them: to put them to death. The Bible leaves no room for same-sex lust, even commanding the union between a man and a woman:

> 1 Corinthians 7:2 - Nevertheless, [to avoid] fornication, let every man have his own wife, and let every woman have her own husband.

It is told to us that every woman should have a husband, and every man should have a wife. There is never a mention of men marrying men or women marrying women. The only time sexual interaction is mentioned between these sexes is in condemnation and judgment, and when explaining their origin in reprobation. If we are godly people, we ought to listen to God's word, and understand that the homosexuals are just as bad as murderers and adulterers, and deserve death.

However, some may even attempt to dispute the clear commandment of Leviticus 20:13, which says,

> Leviticus 20:13 - If a man also lie with mankind, as he lieth with a woman, both of them have committed an abomination: they shall surely be put to death; their blood shall be upon them.

"Surely" shall they put to death. However, this is disputed by those false teachers who preach against the law and who claim that this commandment no longer means anything. First of all, regardless of if capital punishment is still in place, we ought to consider the fact that at one point, God called for the death penalty for men who slept with other men, and classified such a sin as an "abomination." Second, it is not so that the law is not in place. In fact, the New Testament repeatedly warns us of our sins, and teaches us to obey God's commandments. Jesus said,

> Matthew 5:17-19 - Think not that I am come to destroy the law, or the prophets: I am not come to destroy, but to fulfil. For verily I say unto you, Till heaven and earth pass, one jot or one tittle shall in no wise

pass from the law, till all be fulfilled. Whosoever therefore shall break one of these least commandments, and shall teach men so, he shall be called the least in the kingdom of heaven: but whosoever shall do and teach them, the same shall be called great in the kingdom of heaven.

Luke 16:14-17 - And the Pharisees also, who were covetous, heard all these things: and they derided him. And he said unto them, Ye are they which justify yourselves before men; but God knoweth your hearts: for that which is highly esteemed among men is abomination in the sight of God. The law and the prophets were until John: since that time the kingdom of God is preached, and every man presseth into it. And it is easier for heaven and earth to pass, than one tittle of the law to fail.

In Jesus's own words, his advent was not to put an end to the law. Those who understand the Gospel understand that salvation has always been by grace through faith. All of the prophets declared witness of this fact (Acts 10:43), and we constantly see mention of salvation through trusting in the Lord in Old Testament books such as Psalms. Instead, the Law is a schoolmaster, which teaches us that we are not worthy of God, and that we thus need a saviour (Romans 3:23, Galatians 3:24). Those who are saved are still expected by God to obey his word. Those who refuse will be chastised and will have a diminished reward in the kingdom of heaven, as the Bible says,

1 Corinthians 6:9-10 - Know ye not that the unrighteous shall not inherit the kingdom of God? Be not deceived: neither fornicators, nor idolaters, nor adulterers, nor effeminate, nor abusers of themselves with mankind, Nor thieves, nor covetous, nor drunkards, nor revilers, nor extortioners, shall inherit the kingdom of God.

The same principle is shown in Galatians 5:19-21 and Revelation 22:14-15, that only those who obey God's commandments will receive an inheritance in God's kingdom. So, even for those who are saved and have eternal life, even though they are saved by grace through faith only, they still have a responsibility to be obedient. The Bible even states that faith does not make the law void, saying,

Romans 3:31 - Do we then make void the law through faith? God forbid: yea, we establish the law.

Later in the same book, Paul tells us that just because we receive grace from God, this is not an excuse or license to sin:

> Romans 6:1-2 - What shall we say then? Shall we continue in sin, that grace may abound? God forbid. How shall we, that are dead to sin, live any longer therein?

The law is good, and it is righteous. This is one of the central messages of the Bible. "Thy law is truth (Psalm 119:142)." It in every way represents the righteousness of God, and shows us that we are sinners. The Bible also says concerning the law,

> 1 Timothy 1:8-10 - But we know that the law is good, if a man use it lawfully; Knowing this, that the law is not made for a righteous man, but for the lawless and disobedient, for the ungodly and for sinners, for unholy and profane, for murderers of fathers and murderers of mothers, for manslayers, For whoremongers, for them that defile themselves with mankind, for menstealers, for liars, for perjured persons, and if there be any other thing that is contrary to sound doctrine;

Those who transgress God's will are taught the law so that they may know what God wishes us to do, and so that we can walk down the road to perfection. To say that the law is done away with because of grace is heresy, and a denial of God's word. The teachers who say such are throwing out God's commands and replacing it with what they perceive to be true liberty. However, the Bible tells us that the liberty which we have in Christ is not the freedom to be wicked. This shall be shown momentarily. In reality, the only thing in the law which has changed are the animal sacrifices (Hebrews 7:12), but this is simply because they are useless on account of the sacrifice of Christ.

So, just as the law is not abolished, neither is the death penalty. If we were to live in a godly nation with a God-fearing, righteous government, we would set forth God's commands over man's philosophies and execute those who commit homosexuality. In fact, this is the nature and purpose of government in the first place; to punish evildoers. The Bible says,

> Romans 13:1-7 - Let every soul be subject unto the higher powers. For there is no power but of God: the powers that be are ordained of God.

Whosoever therefore resisteth the power, resisteth the ordinance of God: and they that resist shall receive to themselves damnation. For rulers are not a terror to good works, but to the evil. Wilt thou then not be afraid of the power? do that which is good, and thou shalt have praise of the same: For he is the minister of God to thee for good. But if thou do that which is evil, be afraid; for he beareth not the sword in vain: for he is the minister of God, a revenger to execute wrath upon him that doeth evil. Wherefore ye must needs be subject, not only for wrath, but also for conscience sake. For for this cause pay ye tribute also: for they are God's ministers, attending continually upon this very thing. Render therefore to all their dues: tribute to whom tribute is due; custom to whom custom; fear to whom fear; honour to whom honour.

A godly government is ordained of God, just as the government of ancient Israel did not rule except by God's power. It was God himself who set up Saul, and later David, over the children of Israel. God has created the ordinance of government to place human rulers over humans, as means of executing judgment upon those who do evil. In verse 3, it says "For rulers are not a terror to good works, but to the evil," meaning that, a nation's leader is meant to be terrifying to those who commit evil deeds. The Bible furthermore says,

1 Peter 2:13-17 - Submit yourselves to every ordinance of man for the Lord's sake: whether it be to the king, as supreme; <u>Or unto governors, as unto them that are sent by him for the punishment of evildoers,</u> and for the praise of them that do well. For so is the will of God, that with well doing ye may put to silence the ignorance of foolish men<u>: As free, and not using your liberty for a cloke of maliciousness</u>, but as the servants of God. Honour all men. Love the brotherhood. Fear God. Honour the king.

This passage directly states that governors and kings are set up for the punishment of evildoers. This is the sole purpose of government, to serve God by putting away sin from the people. This is why it says in verse 4 of Romans 13, "for he is the minister of God, a revenger to execute wrath upon him that doeth evil." We see furthermore in the Book of Ezra that a commandment is given for the king to use any punishment necessary to put those who disobey God into order, which includes execution (7:25-26). Do not be deceived by the libertarian philosophies of the world. Our liberty is not absolute, it does not mean we can simply do whatever we want. When we break God's law, not only will God curse us, but these curses will be carried out through the wrath of the ordinance of government.

Thus, if the government bears the sword to execute judgment upon evildoers, it is the role of a good, godly government, to execute homosexuals, as the Bible commands. The principle of capital punishment has been in place since the time of the flood, a way to quarantine wickedness. The Bible says,

> Genesis 9:6 - Whoso sheddeth man's blood, by man shall his blood be shed: for in the image of God made he man.

We should not expect God to do all of the work when it comes to destruction of evil. God has commanded us to shed the blood of men ourselves for their sins. This is how the world works. And this is what we see throughout the Law of Moses as well. The phrase "put to death", as it appears in Leviticus 20:13, is not merely a statement of God's wrath. Rather, it is a commandment towards us to execute these homosexuals through the institution of government. The fact that this is telling mankind to put them to death is revealed through a simple reading of the Law. It is written,

> Leviticus 20:10 - And the man that committeth adultery with another man's wife, even he that committeth adultery with his neighbour's wife, the adulterer and the adulteress shall surely be put to death.

> Deuteronomy 22:22-24 - If a man be found lying with a woman married to an husband, then they shall both of them die, both the man that lay with the woman, and the woman: so shalt thou put away evil from Israel. If a damsel that is a virgin be betrothed unto an husband, and a man find her in the city, and lie with her; Then ye shall bring them both out unto the gate of that city, and ye shall stone them with stones that they die; the damsel, because she cried not, being in the city; and the man, because he hath humbled his neighbour's wife: so thou shalt put away evil from among you.

In Leviticus 20:10, the same language which is used 3 verses later appears, telling us that adulterers and adulteresses shall be put to death. However, this is not a statement telling us simply that God is going to execute wrath upon him, as is shown by Deuteronomy 22. In this chapter, it's stated directly that

"YE shall bring them both out unto the gate of that city, and YE shall stone them with stones that they die." So, we see the purpose of the government coming into effect here, in that we are directly commanded to execute judgment upon them ourselves. Thus we see that adulterers are put to death through man, so that we put away the evil among us. It is further written:

> Leviticus 24:17 - And he that killeth any man shall surely be put to death. (Genesis 9:6)

> Exodus 21:12-14 - He that smiteth a man, so that he die, shall be surely put to death. And if a man lie not in wait, but God deliver him into his hand; then I will appoint thee a place whither he shall flee. But if a man come presumptuously upon his neighbour, to slay him with guile; thou shalt take him from mine altar, that he may die.

Thus we see another example of how the Bible tells us that a murderer shall "surely be put to death", and elsewhere shows us that it's God's intention for us to drag these murderers away from God's altar to execute him. This is again shown with bestialiters,

> Exodus 22:19 - Whosoever lieth with a beast shall surely be put to death.

> Leviticus 20:15 - And if a man lie with a beast, he shall surely be put to death: and ye shall slay the beast. And if a woman approach unto any beast, and lie down thereto, thou shalt kill the woman, and the beast: they shall surely be put to death; their blood shall be upon them.

This is also shown with those who are witches:

> Exodus 22:18 - Thou shalt not suffer a witch to live.

> Leviticus 20:27 - A man also or woman that hath a familiar spirit, or that is a wizard, shall surely be put to death: they shall stone them with stones: their blood shall be upon them.

So, the Bible repeatedly shows us over and over again that the meaning of "put to death" is that we are to execute them, to put them to death ourselves. Why should it be any different in Leviticus 20:13, when the entire chapter constantly calls for the execution of others who commit horrific sins, such as bestiality, adultery, and witchcraft, among others? Have understanding: the

Bible says "they shall surely be put to death; their blood shall be upon them" in reference to those men who lie with other men. Simply put: homosexuals deserve the death penalty! This is what God has spoken.

We must understand that God has rejected these homosexuals. They do not matter, they are become worthless. The very first direct mention of reprobation in the Bible is this:

> Jeremiah 6:30 - Reprobate silver shall men call them, because the LORD hath rejected them.

Those who are reprobates have been rejected by God. Homosexuals have been rejected by God. As it teaches in Judges 19 with the men of Gibeah, they are "sons of Belial", or "sons of worthlessness." They have been given over and given up already. Once they have gotten to this point, and manifest it by their wicked sins, it is our duty to put them to death. This is not to go out and take justice into our own hands by killing them individually. Rather, it is an institutional action. If a magistracy which followed the Bible was in place, it should obey this commandment. Such shall be when Jesus Christ comes back, when he shall rule over the earth with a rod of iron (Rev. 2:27).

These people are under a curse. God promised judgment upon the wickedness of the world. We have seen this already in the case of Sodom and Gomorrah, which was set as an example (Jude 1:7), and through various other stories and warning prophecies in the Bible (such as that in the Book of Amos). However, the Bible also specifically gives us lists of curses which shall come upon people if they refuse to obey God's commandments. These examples not only are over the sodomite today, but also on those nations which support those sodomites. The Bible says,

> Deuteronomy 28:15 - But it shall come to pass, if thou wilt not hearken unto the voice of the Lord thy God, to observe to do all his commandments and his statutes which I command thee this day; that all these curses shall come upon thee, and overtake thee:

This introduction precedes 50+ more verses listing these curses which God promised to bring upon Israel for disobeying his commandments and statutes. We see among the list:

Deuteronomy 28:22 - The Lord shall smite thee with a consumption, and with a fever, and with an inflammation, and with an extreme burning, and with the sword, and with blasting, and with mildew; and they shall pursue thee until thou perish.

Deuteronomy 28:59-61 - Then the Lord will make thy plagues wonderful, and the plagues of thy seed, even great plagues, and of long continuance, and sore sicknesses, and of long continuance. Moreover he will bring upon thee all the diseases of Egypt, which thou wast afraid of; and they shall cleave unto thee. Also every sickness, and every plague, which is not written in the book of this law, them will the Lord bring upon thee, until thou be destroyed.

So, God promises to bring plagues, and sicknesses, and all kinds of diseases upon those who disobey his word. This is one of the ways in which God unleashes his wrath. We see examples of this throughout the Bible:

Numbers 25:9 - <u>And Israel abode in Shittim, and the people began to commit whoredom with the daughters of Moab. And they called the people unto the sacrifices of their gods: and the people did eat, and bowed down to their gods</u>. And Israel joined himself unto Baalpeor: and the anger of the LORD was kindled against Israel. And the LORD said unto Moses, Take all the heads of the people, and hang them up before the LORD against the sun, that the fierce anger of the LORD may be turned away from Israel. And Moses said unto the judges of Israel, Slay ye every one his men that were joined unto Baalpeor. And, behold, one of the children of Israel came and brought unto his brethren a Midianitish woman in the sight of Moses, and in the sight of all the congregation of the children of Israel, who were weeping before the door of the tabernacle of the congregation. And when Phinehas, the son of Eleazar, the son of Aaron the priest, saw it, he rose up from among the congregation, and took a javelin in his hand; And he went after the man of Israel into the tent, and thrust both of them through, the man of Israel, and the woman through her belly. So the plague was stayed from the children of Israel. <u>And those that died in the plague were twenty and four thousand.</u>

Here we see an example of God's judgment on people who commit fornication and idolatry. Those who turn from the Lord will sometimes be inflicted with plagues and diseases. God promised this multiple other times in the Bible, that one of the punishments of sin is disease, saying,

> Leviticus 26:14-16 - But if ye will not hearken unto me, and will not do all these commandments; And if ye shall despise my statutes, or if your soul abhor my judgments, so that ye will not do all my commandments, but that ye break my covenant: I also will do this unto you; I will even appoint over you terror, consumption, and the burning ague, that shall consume the eyes, and cause sorrow of heart: and ye shall sow your seed in vain, for your enemies shall eat it.

> 2 Chronicles 21:18-19 - And after all this the LORD smote him in his bowels with an incurable disease. And it came to pass, that in process of time, after the end of two years, his bowels fell out by reason of his sickness: so he died of sore diseases. And his people made no burning for him, like the burning of his fathers.

> 1 Corinthians 11:29-30 - For he that eateth and drinketh unworthily, eateth and drinketh damnation to himself, not discerning the Lord's body. For this cause many are weak and sickly among you, and many sleep.

These and many other examples show sickness as the judgment of God. The example in 2 Chronicles refers to the wicked king Jehoram, who "walked in the ways of the kings of Israel." For his sin, he eventually died of an incurable disease which the LORD gave to him. This is exactly what has happened to homosexuals. They are under the curse of God today.

There exist a certain class of diseases known as STDs (sexually-transmitted diseases), which are spread mainly through sexual intercourse. Some common STDs include the AIDS and HIV virus, syphilis, and gonorrhea, among others. The fact of the matter is, many of these STDs, especially AIDS, are most common among homosexuals, and are themselves judgments of God against these reprobates. On a 2017 Gallup poll, 4.1% of American adults identified as "LGBT" (Gary Gates, "In US, More Adults Identifying as LGBT). However, despite this low percentage of the overall population, according to the CDC, 67% of all HIV diagnoses in 2016 were among gay and bisexual men (cdc.gov, "HIV and Gay and Bisexual Men"). In 2010, it was estimated by the CDC that 78% of all men with HIV were homosexuals.

According to the HIV Bureau, homosexuals were between 44 and 86 times more likely to be infected with AIDS than heterosexuals (HIV/AIDS Bureau, "Gay Men and the History of the Ryan White HIV/AIDS Program").

For this reason, AIDS used to be known by another name, when it was discovered in 1981. Before being titled "Acquired Immune Deficiency Syndrome", the disease was called GRID (Gay-Related Immune Deficiency). This disease was discovered in June of 1981 among 5 homosexual men, prior to a massive outbreak of the disease in the 1980s. It was soon discovered also that those who have acquired the HIV virus were subject to a symptom known as Kaposi's sarcoma (a type of cancer which causes skin lesions), which appeared widely among young homosexuals (Friedman-Kien AE, October 1981, "Disseminated Kaposi's sarcoma syndrome in young homosexual men", *Journal of the American Academy of Dermatology*). The disease only spread to heterosexuals through bisexuals, blood transfusions, and the use of drugs. Sodomites with AIDS who also poked themselves with needles would leave these dirty needles lying around cities like San Francisco, causing the disease to spread. In addition, some homosexuals would donate blood to hospitals despite knowing that they had AIDS, which only spread the disease further.

The effects of the AIDS epidemic caused the city governments of places like San Francisco to shut down gay bathhouses and gay bars (those which hadn't already gone out of business from the loss of their customers to AIDS). Places like these encouraged the spread of the disease. Interviews with eyewitnesses who worked in a meat-packing business near a gay bar called the "Mine Shaft", said in the 80s, "They're making love in the street on top of cars and everything. This is men, grown men. I mean, that's not normal. We've seen it all since we've been here. They try to pick us up. They come out drunk. Sometimes in the morning you see needles on the floor here, and we have to work around it. You see, this is government meat inspected places here." I encourage the reader to go and watch old news interviews and investigations which came out of the AIDS crisis. Many of these had been compiled for the documentary by Pastor Steven Anderson, called "AIDS: The Judgment of God", which I also recommend.

HIV/AIDS is a serious issue. Over 36.9 million people worldwide are affected by this disease. It is estimated that 1.9 million die worldwide a year from this disease, and that there have been over 30 million deaths from AIDS since

1981 when the disease was first discovered (Global Report Fact Sheet" (PDF). UNAIDS. 2010). Symptoms include fevers, rashes, muscle aches, a sore throat, swollen lymph nodes, mouth ulcers, and fatigue as HIV. When AIDS develops and the immune system weakens (AIDS being "Acquired Immune Deficiency Syndrome", HIV being the virus which causes the syndrome), symptoms can include rapid weight loss, diarrhea, memory loss, sores on the genitals, and extreme tiredness (hiv.gov, "How Can You Tell If You Have HIV"). This is a serious sickness.

The CDC also estimates that 80.6% of all syphilis cases are among the group called "MSM", which stands for "men who have sex with men". In other words, sodomites (cdc.gov, "STDs in Men Who Have Sex with Other Men"). In 2014, MSMs accounted for 83% of syphilis diagnoses (cdc.gov, "Sexually Transmitted Diseases). This same article also states that gay men are 17 times more likely to get anal cancer than heterosexuals. In 2015, 38% of all gonorrhea cases were among MSM. The rate of chlamydia positivity among lesbian women is 7.1%, compared to 0.6% for women overall (Linda M. Gorgos, "Sexually Transmitted Infections Among Women Who Have Sex With Women").

Additionally, despite what the media may try to brainwash you with, the idea of 'gay marriage' is rare, as the majority of homosexuals have had multiple partners, and sleep with complete strangers. A 1978 study by Bell and Weinberg shows that 28% of homosexual men admitted to sleeping with over 1000 partners, 43% with 500 or more, and 83% with 50 or more. Only 4% of all MSM even claimed to be faithful to a single partner. In addition, 79% of those studied said that over half of these partners were complete strangers. (Bell and Weinberg, pg. 308-309). This is one of the causes of why epidemics like AIDS spread so quickly in the 1980s. The sodomite lifestyle is dangerous in other ways. In a study of 2000 lesbian women, 75% were found to have pursued psychological counselling for long-term depression (J. Bradford, "National Lesbian Health Care Survey: Implications for Mental Health Care," *Journal of Consulting and Clinical Psychology* 62 (1994): 239, cited in Health Implications Associated with Homosexuality, pg. 81.)

Homosexual men were also found to be 6 times more likely to have committed suicide than heterosexuals (Study by Bell and Weinberg, "Homosexualities", Table 21.12). Studies also indicate that between 25% and 33% of homosexuals are alcoholics, compared with 7% for the general population

(Robert J. Kus, "Alcoholics Anonymous and Gay American Men," *Journal of Homosexuality*, Volume 14, No.2 (1987), pg. 254). 90% of lesbians reported having received verbal abuse from their partners, and 31% reported physical abuse (Lettie L. Lockhart, "Letting out the Secret: Violence in Lesbian Relationships," *Journal of Interpersonal Violence* 9 (1994)). In addition, domestic violence among gay men is twice as much as in the heterosexual population (Gwat Yong Lie and Sabrina Gentlewarrier, "Intimate Violence in Lesbian Relationships: Discussion of Survey Findings and Practice Implications," *Journal of Social Service Research* 15 (1991)). The life expectancy of gay men is between 8 and 20 years lower than that of the heterosexual population (Robert S. Hogg, "Modeling the Impact of HIV Disease on Mortality in Gay and Bisexual Men," *International Journal of Epidemiology* 26 (1997): 657). 29% of the adopted children of homosexual parents experience molestation by their parents, compared to 0.6% of children under heterosexual parents. This means that homosexual parents are 50 times more likely to molest their children (P. Cameron and K. Cameron, "Homosexual Parents," Adolescence 31 (1996): 772).

To say that being a sodomite is a normal, healthy lifestyle is beyond a mere lie. It is complete delusion. These people's lives are disgusting and miserable, filled with alcoholism, abuse, drugs, and disease - disease which come from God as a judgment against their wickedness. Do not let the world deceive you. Being a faggot is not normal, it is not healthy, it is not safe. Those who become these reprobates are cursed by God, and that is a fact. The Bible promises that God will bring these curses upon the wicked, and we see that this is the case for sodomites. It's no coincidence that one of the states where AIDS had the most devastating effect - California, repealed laws against sodomy only 5 years before the outbreak began, in 1976.

However, this is not what the world tells you. The world, allied with Satan, deceives you into thinking that homosexuality is not sinful, that there's no big deal with homosexuality. Since Illinois, the first state to repeal its sodomy laws, did so in 1962, we've seen a progressive decline towards complete degeneracy in the United States. Propaganda supporting the lies of the sodomites have been shoved down our throats through movies, music, television, and the decisions of lawmakers. We ought to discern the truth.

We have already seen an example of how homosexual propaganda is false in the case of the studies of sodomite promscuity. The media may profess a lot about "same-sex marriage", but in reality, the majority of sodomites do not wish to be engaged in a single relationship. They want to sleep with strangers, to be "without natural affection." We also see major corporations like Google and Apple changing their logos during pride month to support the gays. In 2015, prior to the Supreme Court Obergefell v. Hodges decision, a total of 379 companies voiced their support for the legalization of same-sex marriage. These companies include Coca-Cola, Google, Ben & Jerry's, Goldman Sachs bank, Amazon, AT&T, Microsoft, Target, among other well-known groups (Alexander C. Kaufmann, "Here Are The 379 Companies Urging The Supreme Court To Support Same-Sex Marriage," *The Huffington Post*).

In 2017, London council block planners insisted that a new block of flats must have a gay bar as a condition of the development, in which workers would be sent to see if the bar was LGBT friendly (August 5th, 2017, Charlie Moore, *mailonline*). In February 2019, New Jersey adopted a law requiring public schools to teach LGBT history (Hannan Adley, "New Jersey becomes second state in nation to require that schools teach LGBT history", *North Jersey Record*). Some schools are even forcing children to learn about the act of sodomy itself (Katie Jerkovich, "California School District Says Parents Can't Pull Kids Out of New LGBT Sex-Ed Class," *The Daily Caller*). In 2016, the Unruh Civil Rights Act in California forced religious dating sites like Christian Mingle and LDS Singles to include LGBT singles (Kelsey Dallas, "Christian Mingle, other religious dating sites must now serve LGBT singles," *Deseret News* and *Washington Times*). A Jewish private school was criticized in the UK for not teaching LGBT issues (Olivia Rudgard, "Private religious school fails third Ofsted inspection because it does not teach about LGBT issues," *The Telegraph*). Bewsey Lodge Primary School in England taught children as young as 6 to write gay love letters to each other (Calvin Freiburger, "6-year-olds forced to write gay 'love letters' to teach 'accepting diversity',"*Lifesite News*).

Folks, it's obvious that homosexuality is not only accepted by society, but that it's being forced upon us. Where public school districts used to promote PSAs warning children about sodomites, they now are openly teaching LGBT propaganda to children. This is just them forcing lies down our throat, preparing the next generation to become even more wicked than our own.

One of the other lies which the sodomites might say is that they were "born that way." This is an attempt at defending their behavior. Often homosexuals will come up with the objection of "If God hates us, why did he create us?" However, God did not create homosexuals. Nobody is born gay. This is what the Bible teaches, first of all. This has already been addressed. People become homosexuals because they reject God's truth and turn towards false gods and religions. In hardening their hearts, they are given over to a reprobate mind, and their conscience becomes defiled. This is acquired, it is not an inherent trait of some people.

This is also confirmed by science. There has never been any genetic link discovered to homosexuality. In fact, studies among identical twins prove that homosexuality is not genetic. Identical twins are monozygotic, meaning that they are produced from the same zygote (a union of the sperm and egg), and that they thus have the same exact genetic makeup. Dr. Neil Whitehead, a scientific researcher for the New Zealand government and a member of the United Nations and International Atomic Energy Agency, published a study in 2013 showing that there is only an 11% chance for men, and 14% for women, that if one identical twin is a homosexual, the other will be as well. Since they're identical twins, this number should be 100%. But it's not (Mark Ellis, "Identical Twins Studies Prove Homosexuality is Not Genetic," *The Aquila Report*). A 2000 study by Bailey, Dunne, and Martin show similar numbers (Bailey, J.M., Dunne, M.P., & Martin, N.G. (2000), "Genetic and Environmental influences on sexual orientation and its correlates in an Australian twin sample," *Journal of Personality and Social Psychology*, 78, 524-536). A 1999 study by Bailey and Pillard found that only 13 out of 41 tested twin subjects shared homosexuality (32%) (Bailey, M, Pillard, R (1991), "A Genetic Study of Male Sexual Orientation," *Archives of General Psychiatry*, 1991, no 48, 1089-1096.). It should be noted that this same study also found that 11% of adopted brothers also shared the same homosexual orientation (despite sharing no genes, thus proving a possible link to environmental factors).

Thus, there's no proof that homosexuals are born as homosexuals. In fact, all evidence points to the exact opposite, that one becomes a sodomite later in their life.

Another example of homosexual lies which you might hear from the world is that they're innocent, that they're just ordinary people like us. This, again, is refuted by the Biblical statement "being filled with all unrighteousness." Reprobates have no filter. They have no moral compass, and thus, they enter into a multitude of sins. One of these sins is pedophilia. The world may try to deny it, but the majority of sodomites, if not all, are not only attracted to the same-sex, but they are attracted to children as well. How do I know? First of all, because the Bible says:

> Romans 1:29-31 - Being filled with all unrighteousness, fornication, wickedness, covetousness, maliciousness; full of envy, murder, debate, deceit, malignity; whisperers, Backbiters, haters of God, despiteful, proud, boasters, inventors of evil things, disobedient to parents, Without understanding, covenantbreakers, without natural affection, implacable, unmerciful:

This does not say "filled with some unrighteousness." Among the sins listed are fornication and being "without natural affection," meaning that they are attracted to things which are not natural. A normal person does not become a pedophile. It's disgusting, against all reasoning. Jesus said,

> Matthew 18:2-14 - And Jesus called a little child unto him, and set him in the midst of them, And said, Verily I say unto you, Except ye be converted, and become as little children, ye shall not enter into the kingdom of heaven. Whosoever therefore shall humble himself as this little child, the same is greatest in the kingdom of heaven. And whoso shall receive one such little child in my name receiveth me. <u>But whoso shall offend one of these little ones which believe in me, it were better for him that a millstone were hanged about his neck, and that he were drowned in the depth of the sea</u>. Woe unto the world because of offences! for it must needs be that offences come; but woe to that man by whom the offence cometh! Wherefore if thy hand or thy foot offend thee, cut them off, and cast them from thee: it is better for thee to enter into life halt or maimed, rather than having two hands or two feet to be cast into everlasting fire. And if thine eye offend thee, pluck it out, and cast it from thee: it is better for thee to enter into life with one eye, rather than having two eyes to be cast into hell fire. <u>Take heed that ye despise not one of these little ones</u>; for I say unto you, That in heaven their angels do always behold the face of my Father which is in heaven. For the Son of man is come to save that which was lost. How think ye? if a man have an hundred sheep, and one of them be gone astray, doth he not leave the ninety and nine, and goeth into the mountains, and seeketh that which is gone astray? And if so be that he find it, verily I

say unto you, he rejoiceth more of that sheep, than of the ninety and nine which went not astray. Even so it is not the will of your Father which is in heaven, that one of these little ones should perish.

To abuse children is one of the most wicked things somebody could do. And it just so happens that the facts show that the majority of homosexuals are pedophiles as well. A study known as "The Gay Report", published in 1979 by homosexual researchers Karla Young and Allen Jay, reported that 73% of homosexuals interviewed admitted to having sex with boys between the ages of 16 and 19 or YOUNGER. A study by Dr. Paul Cameron in 1983 found that 30% of child molestations were homosexual encounters (Cameron, et al (1986) "Child molestation and homosexuality," Psychological Rpts 58:327-37). A 1984 study found also that in Los Angeles, 35% of child molestations were by homosexuals (Siegal, et al (1987), "The prevalence of childhood sexual assault," American J Epidemiology 126:1141-53). A random study of British teens showed that 35% of boys and 9% of girls were molested by homosexuals (Schofield (1965), "The sexual behaviour of young people"). At the Massachusetts Treatment Center for Sexually Dangerous Persons, it was found that a third of the child molesters were homosexuals (Eastern Psych Assn Convention (1991) Interview with Dr. Raymond A. Knight at his presentation, Differential prevalence of personality disorders in rapists and child molesters. New York, April 12).

Of the 52 convicted child molesters in Ottawa, Canada from 1983 to 1985, 60% were found to be homosexuals (Bradford, et al (1988), "The heterogeneity/homogeneity of pedophilia," Psychiatric J Univ Ottawa 13:217-26). At the Kingston's Sexual Behaviour Clinic, 38 of the 91 child molesters (42%) were homosexuals (Marshall, et al (1991), "Early onset and deviant sexuality in child molesters," J Interpersonal Violence 6:323-36). The list of scientific studies could go on. This is no coincidence. Despite making up only 3-4% of the population, homosexuals represent over a third of child molestation cases. If bisexuals are factored in, this increases to nearly two-thirds of all child molesters. That means that sodomites are nearly 50 times more likely to molest children than heterosexuals. Do not be deceived. Sodomites and pedophiles are synonymous.

It's not a coincidence that there are currently over 3,000 cases of child molestation by Catholic priests. These priests, who have had the Bible in their hands for years, despite having received the truth, remain in the religion of

Mystery Babylon and reject the true Gospel. This is what leads them to their horrific treatment of children. Homosexuals are filthy, unclean people, and the Bible says "Who can bring a clean thing out of an unclean? Not one" (Job 14:4).

Warning: if what has been discussed isn't disgusting enough, what is about to be discussed is perhaps even more perplexing. When the Bible says that they are filled with all unrighteousness, this includes uncleanness, which is a work of the flesh according to Galatians 5:19-21. Homosexuals often engage in other filthy acts such as: ingesting feces. A study showed that 80% of gays admitted to consuming the feces of their partners (Corey & Holmes (1980), "Sexual transmission of Hepatitis A in homosexual men," New England J Medicine 302:435-38). This same study found that on average, gays admitted to consuming the fecal matter of partners at least 19 times annually. A report from the San Francisco Department of Public Health in the 1970s found that among a group of 75,000 people who had contracted hepatitis A, shigella, giardia, or other infections from consuming fecal matter, 70-80% were homosexuals.

The 1979 "Gay Report" by Jay and Young mentioned earlier, also found that 23% of homosexuals engaged in sex involving urine. Dr. Paul Cameron found in his study that 29% of gays engaged in urine-sex (Cameron, et al (1985), "Sexual orientation and sexually transmitted disease," Nebraska Medical J 70:292-99; (1989), "The effect of homosexuality upon public health and social order," Psychological Rpts 64:1167-79). One study during the early days of the AIDS crisis found that 90% of gays admitted to using illegal drugs (Jafee, et al (1983), "National case-control study of Kaposi's sarcoma," Annals Internal Medicine 99:145-51). Another study found this number at 45% (Rotheram-Borus, et al (1994), "Sexual and substance abuse acts of gay and bisexual male adolescents," J Sex Research 31:47-57).

You look me in the eye and tell me that eating feces, pissing on your sex partner, doing drugs, going after children, and contracting multitudes of deadly diseases is a "normal, healthy lifestyle." It is not a lifestyle, it is a deathstyle.

Conclusion

In this essay, we have seen beyond a shadow of a doubt that there are certain people who hate God and reject his clear truth of the Gospel. Upon hardening their hearts and shutting up their ears to the truth, they are given over to a reprobate mind. Their conscience is defiled, and they are given up to uncleanness and vile affections. This state, known as "reprobation", is synonymous with the medical term "psychopath." Sodomites are included in this category. The reason why men lust after men, and women lust after other women in the first place, is because they have become reprobates. They thus become worthless, wicked sinners above ordinary unbelievers, filled with all unrighteousness, who deserve nothing but death. Homosexuals are violent abusers, drug users, pedophiles, unclean, filthy animals, deceivers, rapists, drunkards, haters of God.

This is the truth. So, what should we do with this information? Do as the Bible instructs: "from such turn away" (2 Timothy 3:5). Stay away from these people before they lead us down into the path of hell as well. What else? Let's keep the homosexuals out of our churches and away from our children. And most importantly, let's keep people from turning to the path of darkness by obeying Jesus' command in Mark 16:15 - Go ye into all the world, and preach the Gospel to every creature." In other words, lead people to the Lord, get them saved, before it's too late. Show them the true Gospel, before a false prophet gets to them. Let's do everything in our power to win this spiritual war. The Bible says:

> Ephesians 6:12 - For we wrestle not against flesh and blood, but against principalities, against powers, against the rulers of the darkness of this world, against spiritual wickedness in high places.

We can't let Satan win this fight. Reject degeneracy and obey the word of the Lord. Amen.

Lightning Source UK Ltd.
Milton Keynes UK
UKHW041838090620
364729UK00001B/28

9 780359 736522